Crocheted Slippers for women & children

CONTENTS

LEISURE ARTS, INC. • Maumelle, Arkansas

GENERAL INSTRUCTIONS

ABBREVIATIONS

approx	approximately
beg	begin(ning)
BLO	back loop only
ch(s)	chain(s)
dc	double crochet(s)
dec	decrease(ing)
est	established
hdc	half double crochet(s)
inc	increase(ing)
prev	previous
rem	remain(ing)
rep	repeat
rnd(s)	round(s)
sc	single crochet(s)
sk	skip
sl st(s)	slip stitch(es)
sp	space(s)
st(s)	stitch(es)
tog	together
YO	yarn over

SYMBOLS & TERMS

★ or ★★ – work instructions following ★ or ★★ as many **more** times as indicated in addition to the first time.

( ) or **[ ]** – work enclosed instructions **as many** times as specified by the number immediately following **or** work all enclosed instructions in the stitch or space indicated **or** contains explanatory remarks.

work even – work without increasing or decreasing in pattern established

GAUGE

Correct gauge is essential for proper size of garments. Hook sizes given in instructions are merely guides and should never be used without first making a swatch to check gauge. To test gauge, make a sample swatch approx 4" in the stitch, yarn and hook specified. Then measure it, counting your stitches and rows carefully. If you have more stitches per inch than specified, try again with a larger size hook; if fewer, try again with a smaller size. Keep trying until you find the size that will give you the specified gauge. **DO NOT HESITATE TO CHANGE HOOK SIZE TO OBTAIN CORRECT GAUGE.**

WASHING

Slippers with plastic canvas inserts are washable, but should be air dried. Plastic canvas CANNOT be professionally dry cleaned or put in the clothes dryer.

CONVERSION CHART		
1 ounce	=	28.4 grams
$1^1/_2$ ounces	=	42.6 grams
2 ounces	=	56.8 grams
$3^1/_2$ ounces	=	99.4 grams
4 ounces	=	113.6 grams

CROCHET HOOKS																
U.S.	B-1	C-2	D-3	E-4	F-5	G-6	7	H-8	I-9	J-10	K-10½	L-11	M/N-13	N/P-15	P/Q	Q	S
Metric - mm	2.25	2.75	3.25	3.5	3.75	4	4.5	5	5.5	6	6.5	8	9	10	15	16	19

1. FUZZY SLIPPER

Shown on front cover

designed by Modene Thornton; Little Rock, AR

WOMEN'S SIZES:	**SMALL**	**MEDIUM**	**LARGE**
	9"	9½"	10"

MATERIALS

Worsted wt yarn – 5(6-7) oz
[approx 142(176-199.5) grams] Blue

Aluminum crochet hook –
Size G (4.5 mm) **for size Small only**
Size H (5.5 mm) **for size Medium only**
Size I (6 mm) **for size Large only**
or size needed for gauge

Tapestry or yarn needle

GAUGE: Size G hook, 16 sc and 16 rows = 4"
Size H hook, 14 sc and 14 rows = 4"
Size I hook, 12 sc and 12 rows = 4"

INSTRUCTIONS

SOLE (Make 2)

With crochet hook for desired gauge, ch 26 **loosely**.

Rnd 1: Work 2 sc in 2nd ch from hook **(inc made)**, sc in each of next 10 chs, hdc in each of next 3 chs, dc in each of next 8 chs, 2 dc in next ch, hdc in next ch, 5 sc in last ch (toe); turn piece to work in unused loops of foundation ch, hdc in next loop, 2 dc in next loop, dc in each of next 8 loops, hdc in each of next 3 loops, sc in each of next 10 loops, inc in last loop; **do not join**, mark beg of rnd with contrasting yarn **(now and throughout)**: 57 sts.

Rnd 2: Inc in first sc of prev rnd, inc in next sc, sc in each of next 24 sts, (inc in next sc, sc in next sc) twice, inc in next sc, sc in each of next 24 sts, inc in each of rem 2 sc: 64 sc.

Rnd 3: Sc in first sc of prev rnd, inc in next sc, sc in each of next 25 sc, (inc in next sc, sc in each of next 2 sc) 3 times, inc in next sc, sc in each of next 25 sc, inc in next sc, sc in last sc: 70 sc.

Rnd 4: Sc in first sc of prev rnd, inc in next sc, sc in each of next 28 sc, (inc in next sc, sc in each of next 2 sc) 3 times, inc in next sc, sc in each of next 28 sc, inc in next sc, sc in last sc: 76 sc.

Rnd 5: Sc in first sc of prev rnd, sc in each of next 34 sc, inc in next sc, sc in each of next 4 sc, inc in next sc, sc in each of next 34 sc, sc in last sc; ch 1, **turn**: 78 sc

TOP

Note: **Wrong** side of sole is facing you and slipper is worked inside out.

Rnd 1: Insert hook into first st, wrap yarn around index finger of left hand once, following direction indicated by arrow ***(Fig. 1a)***, hook loop around finger being careful to hook both threads ***(Fig. 1b)***, draw both threads thru st ***(Fig. 1c)***, remove finger from loop, YO and draw thru all 3 loops on hook (**Loop Stitch made**), loop st in each st around; mark beg of rnd with contrasting yarn **(now and throughout)**: 78 loop sts.

Fig. 1a

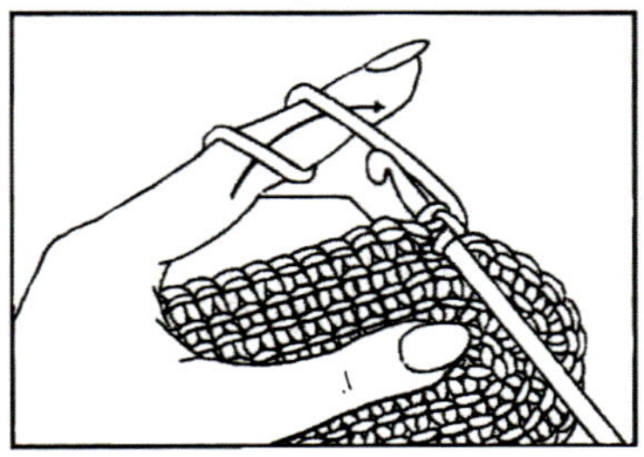

Fig. 1b

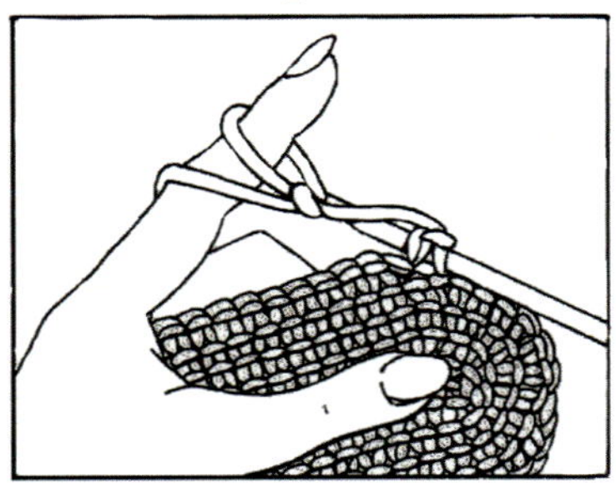

Fig. 1c

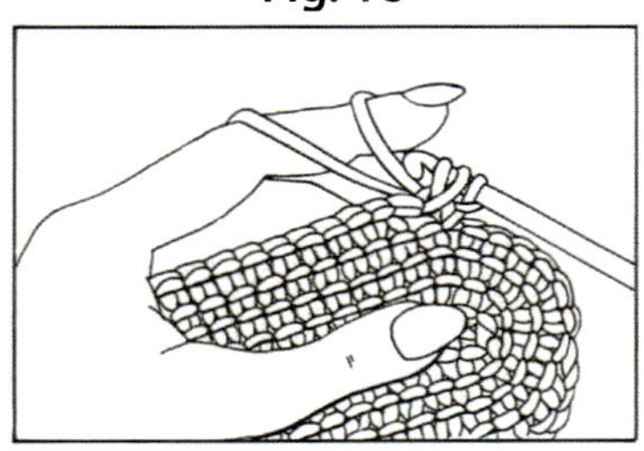

Rnd 2: Loop st in first loop st of prev rnd and in each loop st around.

Rnds 3-10: Rep Rnd 2, 8 times **more**.

Rnd 11: Sl st in each loop st around; finish off.

FINISHING

With wrong side facing, weave 3" at top of toe.
Cut all loops and brush to resemble fur.
Weave in any yarn ends.

CHILDREN'S SIZES:	SMALL	MEDIUM	LARGE
	7½"	8"	8½"

MATERIALS

Worsted wt yarn – 4.5(5.5-6.5) oz
[approx 128.3(156.8-185.3) grams] Blue
Aluminum crochet hook –
Size G (4.5 mm) **for size Small only**
Size H (5.5 mm) **for size Medium only**
Size I (6 mm) **for size Large only**
or size needed for gauge
Tapestry or yarn needle

GAUGE: Size G hook, 16 sc and 16 rows = 4"
Size H hook, 14 sc and 14 rows = 4"
Size I hook, 12 sc and 12 rows = 4"

INSTRUCTIONS

SOLE (Make 2)

With crochet hook for desired gauge, ch 22 **loosely**.

Rnd 1: Work 2 sc in 2nd ch from hook **(inc made)**, sc in each of next 8 chs, hdc in each of next 3 chs, dc in each of next 6 chs, 2 dc in next ch, hdc in next ch, 5 sc in last ch (toe); turn piece to work in unused loops of foundation ch, hdc in next loop, 2 dc in next loop, dc in each of next 6 loops, hdc in each of next 3 loops, sc in each of next 8 loops, inc in last loop; **do not join**, mark beg of rnd with contrasting yarn **(now and throughout)**: 49 sts.

Rnd 2: Inc in first sc of prev rnd, inc in next sc, sc in each of next 20 sts, (inc in next sc, sc in next sc) twice, inc in next sc, sc in each of next 20 sts, inc in each of rem 2 sc: 56 sc.

Rnd 3: Sc in first sc of prev rnd, inc in next sc, sc in each of next 21 sc, (inc in next sc, sc in each of next 2 sc) 3 times, inc in next sc, sc in each of next 21 sc, inc in next sc, sc in last sc: 62 sc.

Rnd 4: Sc in first sc of prev rnd, inc in next sc, sc in each of next 24 sc, (inc in next sc, sc in each of next 2 sc) 3 times, inc in next sc, sc in each of next 24 sc, inc in next sc, sc in last sc: 68 sc.

Rnd 5: Sc in first sc of prev rnd, sc in each of next 30 sc, inc in next sc, sc in each of next 4 sc, inc in next sc, sc in each of next 30 sc, sc in last sc; ch 1, **turn**: 70 sc.

TOP

Note: **Wrong** side of sole is facing you and slipper is worked inside out.

Rnd 1: Loop st (***Figs. 1a-c, page 3***) in first sc, loop st in each sc around; mark beg of rnd with contrasting yarn **(now and throughout)**: 70 loop sts.

Rnd 2: Loop st in first loop st of prev rnd and in each loop st around.

Rnds 3-8: Rep Rnd 2, 6 times **more**.

Rnd 9: Sl st in each loop st around; finish off.

FINISHING

With **wrong** side facing, weave 3" at top of toe.
Cut all loops and brush to resemble fur.
Weave in any yarn ends.

2. GRANNY SQUARE SLIPPERS

Shown on front cover

designed by Knit 'N' Purl Shop; Edina, MN

WOMEN'S SIZES:	**SMALL**	**MEDIUM**	**LARGE**
	9"	9½"	10"

Size *Note*: Instructions are written for women's sizes **only**.

MATERIALS

Worsted wt yarn – 45(50-55) yards Coral
60(70-80) yards Lt Green
150(180-290) yards Lt Coral
Aluminum crochet hook –
Size E (3.5 mm) **for sizes Small & Medium only**
Size F (4 mm) **for size Large only**
or size needed for gauge
Tapestry or yarn needle

GAUGE: For size SMALL, with E hook, one square (3 rnds dc + 1 rnd sc) = 3½"
For size MEDIUM, with E hook, one square (3 rnds dc + 1 rnd hdc) = 3¾"
For size LARGE, with F hook, one square (4 rnds dc) = 4½"

INSTRUCTIONS

Following instructions for Basic Granny Square, using appropriate hook and working required number of rounds, make 6 granny squares for **each** slipper.

Work 3 rnds dc + 1 rnd sc for size SMALL; work 3 rnds dc + 1 rnd hdc for size MEDIUM; work 4 rnds dc for size LARGE.

BASIC GRANNY SQUARE (Make 12)

With Coral, ch 3; join with sl st to form a ring.

Rnd 1: Ch 3, 2 dc in ring, ch 1, ★ 3 dc in ring, ch 1; rep from ★ twice; join with sl st in 3rd ch of beg ch-3, finish off.

Rnd 2: With **right** side facing, join Lt Green with sl st in any ch-1 sp; ch 3, (2 dc, ch 1, 3 dc) in same sp, ★ (3 dc, ch 1, 3 dc) in next ch-1 sp; rep from ★ twice; join with sl st in 3rd ch of beg ch-3, finish off.

Rnd 3: With **right** side facing, join Lt Coral with sl st in any ch-1 sp; (ch 3, 2 dc, ch 1, 3 dc) in same sp, ★ 3 dc in next sp between groups for side, (3 dc, ch 1, 3 dc) in next corner ch-1 sp; rep from ★ twice, 3 dc in next side sp; join with sl st in 3rd ch of beg ch-3.

SIZE SMALL ONLY

Rnd 4: Sl st in each of next 2 dc, sl st in corner sp, ch 1, sc in each st and in each ch-1 sp around, working 3 sc in each ch-1 corner sp; join with sl st in first sc, finish off.

SIZE MEDIUM ONLY

Rnd 4: Sl st in each of next 2 dc, sl st in corner sp, ch 2, hdc in each st and in each ch-1 sp around, working 3 hdc in each corner sp; join with sl st in 2nd ch of beg ch-2, finish off.

SIZE LARGE ONLY

Rnd 4: Sl st in each of next 2 dc, sl st in corner sp, (ch 3, 2 dc, ch 1, 3 dc) in same sp, ★ 3 dc in each sp along side, (3 dc, ch 1, 3 dc) in next corner ch-1 sp; rep from ★ twice, ending by working 3 dc in each sp along side; join with sl st in 3rd ch of beg ch-3, finish off.

ALL SIZES – FINISHING

Thread a tapestry needle with yarn to match last round worked. With **right** sides facing and overcasting in back loops only, join two squares along one side.
Join two more squares in same manner, then join the two groups to form a square.
To form heel, join square 5 as shown in **Fig. 2**.
To form toe, join square 6 as in **Fig. 3**.
Assemble second slipper in same manner.
Weave in any yarn ends.

Fig. 2 **Fig. 3**

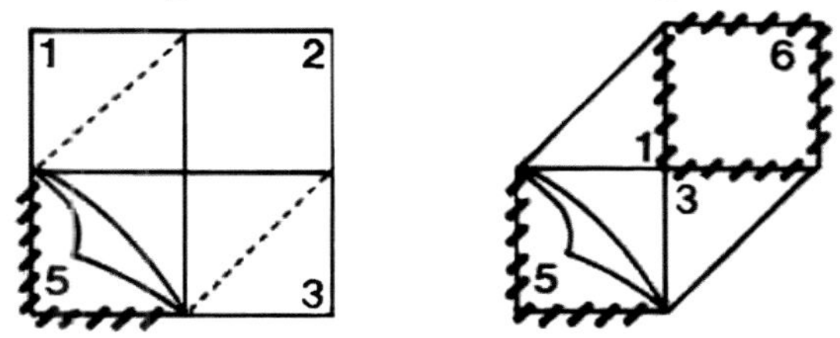

3. FUZZY CUFF

Shown on front cover

designed by Modene Thornton; Little Rock, AR

WOMEN'S SIZES:	SMALL	MEDIUM	LARGE
	9"	9½"	10"

MATERIALS

Worsted wt yarn – 3(3½-4) oz
[approx 85.2(99.4-113.6) grams] Red **and** White
Aluminum crochet hook –
Size G (4.5 mm) **for size Small only**
Size H (5.5 mm) **for size Medium only**
Size I (6 mm) **for size Large only**
or size needed for gauge
Tapestry or yarn needle

GAUGE: Size G hook, 16 sc and 16 rows = 4"
Size H hook, 14 sc and 14 rows = 4"
Size I hook, 12 sc and 12 rows = 4"

INSTRUCTIONS

SOLE (Make 2)

With crochet hook for desired gauge and Red, ch 26 **loosely**.

Rnd 1: Work 2 sc in 2nd ch from hook (**inc made**), sc in each of next 10 chs, hdc in each of next 3 chs, dc in each of next 8 chs, 2 dc in next ch, hdc in next ch, 5 sc in last ch (toe); turn piece to work in unused loops of foundation ch, hdc in next loop, 2 dc in next loop, dc in each of next 8 loops, hdc in each of next 3 loops, sc in each of next 10 loops, inc in last loop; **do not join**, mark beg of rnd with contrasting yarn **(now and throughout)**: 57 sts.

Rnd 2: Inc in first sc of prev rnd, inc in next sc, sc in each of next 24 sts, (inc in next sc, sc in next sc) twice, inc in next sc, sc in each of next 24 sts, inc in each of rem 2 sc: 64 sc.

Rnd 3: Sc in first sc of prev rnd, inc in next sc, sc in each of next 25 sc, (inc in next sc, sc in each of next 2 sc) 3 times, inc in next sc, sc in each of next 25 sc, inc in next sc, sc in last sc: 70 sc.

Rnd 4: Sc in first sc of prev rnd, inc in next sc, sc in each of next 28 sc, (inc in next sc, sc in each of next 2 sc) 3 times, inc in next sc, sc in each of next 28 sc, inc in next sc, sc in last sc: 76 sc.

Rnd 5: Sc in first sc of prev rnd, sc in each of next 34 sc, inc in next sc, sc in each of next 4 sc, inc in next sc, sc in each of next 34 sc, sc in last sc: 78 sc.

SIDES

Rnd 1: Sc in first sc of prev rnd, sc in each sc around.

Rnds 2-6: Rep Rnd 1, 5 times **more**.

Finish off.

TOE INSERT

Row 1: With **right** side facing, join Red with sl st in 34th sc from center sc of heel; ch 3, work dc dec over next 2 sc as follows: (YO, pull up a loop in **next** sc, YO, draw thru 2 loops on hook) twice, YO, draw thru rem 3 loops on hook (**3-dc dec made**), dc in each of next 6 sc, work dc dec over next 3 sc as follows: (YO, pull up a loop in **next** sc, YO, draw thru 2 loops on hook) 3 times, YO, draw thru rem 4 loops on hook **(3-dc dec made)**, sc in last sc; ch 1, **turn**.

Row 2: Sk first sc, sc in 3-dc dec of Insert, sc in each of next 6 dc of Insert, sc in rem 3-dc dec of Insert, (insert hook in **next** sc of Side, pull up a loop) twice, YO and draw thru all 3 loops on hook **(dec made)**; ch 1, turn: 9 sc.

Row 3: Sk first sc, sc in each of next 8 sc of Insert, dec in Side; ch 1, turn.

Row 4: Sk first sc, sc in each of next 8 sc of Insert, sc in next sc of Side; ch 1, turn.

Row 5: Rep Row 4.

Rows 6 and 7: Rep Row 3, twice.

Rows 8 and 9: Rep Row 4, twice.

Rows 10 and 11: Rep Row 3, twice.

Row 12: Rep Row 4; do **not** ch 1, finish off.

CUFF

Rnd 1: With **wrong** side facing, join White with sl st in top of heel; sc in same sc as joining, sc in each of next 23 sc of Side, sc in each of next 8 sc of Toe Insert, sc in each of next 23 sc of Side, sc in last sc; **do not turn**: 57 sc.

Rnd 2: Loop st ***(Figs. 1a-c, page 3)*** in first sc of prev rnd, loop st in each st around: 57 loop sts.

Rnds 3-14: Rep Rnd 2, 12 times **more**.

Rnd 15: Sl st in first loop st of prev rnd and in each loop st around; finish off leaving a 36" length for finishing.

FINISHING

Cut all loops and brush to resemble fur.
With White and tapestry needle, fold Cuff to inside and sew to first Cuff rnd to make hem.
Weave in any yarn ends.

CHILDREN'S SIZES:	SMALL	MEDIUM	LARGE
	7½"	8"	8½"

MATERIALS

Worsted wt yarn – 1½(2-2½) oz
[approx 42.6(56.8-71) grams] Red **and** White
Aluminum crochet hook –
Size G (4.5 mm) **for size Small only**
Size H (5.5 mm) **for size Medium only**
Size I (6 mm) **for size Large only**
or size needed for gauge
Tapestry or yarn needle

GAUGE: Size G hook, 16 sc and 16 rows = 4"
Size H hook, 14 sc and 14 rows = 4"
Size I hook, 12 sc and 12 rows = 4"

INSTRUCTIONS

SOLE (Make 2)

With crochet hook for desired gauge and Red, ch 22 **loosely**.

Rnd 1: Work 2 sc in 2nd ch from hook (**inc made**), sc in each of next 8 chs, hdc in each of next 3 chs, dc in each of next 6 chs, 2 dc in next ch, hdc in next ch, 5 sc in last ch (toe); turn piece to work in unused loops of foundation ch, hdc in next loop, 2 dc in next loop, dc in each of next 6 loops, hdc in each of next 3 loops, sc in each of next 8 loops, inc in last loop; **do not join**, mark beg of rnd with contrasting yarn (**now and throughout**): 49 sts.

Rnd 2: Inc in first sc of prev rnd, inc in next sc, sc in each of next 20 sts, (inc in next sc, sc in next sc) twice, inc in next sc, sc in each of next 20 sts, inc in each of rem 2 sc: 56 sc.

Rnd 3: Sc in first sc of prev rnd, inc in next sc, sc in each of next 21 sc, (inc in next sc, sc in each of next 2 sc) 3 times, inc in next sc, sc in each of next 21 sc, inc in next sc, sc in last sc: 62 sc.

Rnd 4: Sc in first sc of prev rnd, inc in next sc, sc in each of next 24 sc, (inc in next sc, sc in each of next 2 sc) 3 times, inc in next sc, sc in each of next 24 sc, inc in next sc, sc in last sc: 68 sc.

Rnd 5: Sc in first sc of prev rnd, sc in each of next 30 sc, inc in next sc, sc in each of next 4 sc, inc in next sc, sc in each of next 30 sc, sc in last sc: 70 sc.

SIDES

Rnd 1: Sc in first sc of prev rnd, sc in each sc around.

Rnds 2-4: Rep Rnd 1, 3 times **more**.

Finish off.

TOE INSERT

Row 1: With **right** side facing, join Red with sl st in 30th sc from center of heel; ch 3, work dc dec over next 2 sc as follows: (YO, pull up a loop in **next** sc, YO, draw thru 2 loops on hook) twice, YO, draw thru rem 3 loops on hook (**3-dc dec made**), dc in each of next 4 sc, work dc dec over next 3 sc as follows: (YO, pull up a loop in **next** sc, YO, draw thru 2 loops on hook) 3 times, YO, draw thru rem 4 loops on hook) (**3-dc dec made**), sc in last sc; ch 1, **turn**.

Row 2: Sk first sc, sc in 3-dc dec of Insert, sc in each of next 4 dc of Insert, sc in rem 3-dc dec of Insert, (insert hook in **next** sc of Side, pull up a loop) twice, YO and draw thru all 3 loops (**dec made**); ch 1, turn: 7 sc.

Row 3: Sk first sc, sc in each of next 6 sc of Insert, dec in Side; ch 1, turn.

Row 4: Sk first sc, sc in each of next 6 sc of Insert, sc in next sc of Side; ch 1, turn.

Row 5: Rep Row 4.

Rows 6 and 7: Rep Row 3, twice.

Rows 8 and 9: Rep Row 4, twice.

Rows 10 and 11: Rep Row 3, twice; at end of Rnd 11, do **not** ch 1.

Finish off.

CUFF

Rnd 1: With **wrong** side facing, join White with sl st in top of heel; sc in same sc as joining, sc in each of next 20 sc of Side, sc in each of next 7 sc of Toe Insert, sk first sc of Side, sc in each of next 20 sc, sc in last sc; **do not turn**: 49 sc.

Rnd 2: Loop st ***(Figs. 1a-c, page 3)*** in first sc of prev rnd, loop st in each st around: 49 loop sts.

Rnds 3-12: Rep Rnd 2, 10 times **more**.

Rnd 13: Sl st in first loop st of prev rnd and in each loop st around; finish off leaving a 36" length for finishing.

FINISHING

Cut all loops and brush to resemble fur.
With White and tapestry needle, fold Cuff to inside and sew to first Cuff rnd to make hem.
Weave in any yarn ends.

4. CROCHETED MOCCASIN

Shown on back cover
designed by Nancy Sisk

WOMEN'S SIZES:	**SMALL**	**MEDIUM**	**LARGE**
	9"	9½"	10"

Size *Note*: Instructions are written for smallest size with changes for larger sizes in parentheses.

MATERIALS

Worsted wt yarn –
2½(3-3½) oz **[**approx 71(85.2-99.4) grams**]** Dk Blue
2(2½-3) oz **[**approx 56.8(71-85.2) grams**]** Ecru
3 yards Lt Blue
Aluminum crochet hook –
Size E (3.5 mm) **for Top only**
Size G (4.5 mm) **for Sole only**
or sizes needed for gauge
Tapestry or yarn needle

GAUGE: Size E hook, 16 sc and 16 rows = 4"
Size G hook (double strand),
14 sc and 14 rows = 4"

INSTRUCTIONS

SOLE (Make 2)

With larger size hook and **double strand** Dk Blue, ch 22(25-27) **loosely**.

Rnd 1: Work 3 sc in 2nd ch from hook, sc in each of next 9(10-11) chs, dc in each of next 10(12-13) chs, 5 dc in last ch (toe); turn piece to work in each unused loop of foundation ch, dc in each of next 10(12-13) loops, sc in each of rem 10(11-12) loops; mark beg of rnd with contrasting yarn **(now and throughout)**: 47(53-57) sts.

Rnd 2: Work 2 sc in first sc **(inc made)**, inc in next sc (heel), sc in each of next 20(23-25) sts, inc in each of next 5 dc at toe, sc in each of rem 20(23-25) sts: 54(60-64) sc.

Rnd 3: Inc in first sc, sc in next sc, inc in next sc, sc in each of next 21(24-26) sc, (inc in next sc, sc in next sc) 4 times, inc in next sc, sc in each of next 21(24-26) sc: 61(67-71) sc.

SIZE SMALL ONLY

Rnd 4: Sc in first sc and in each of next 15 sc, hdc in each of next 11 sc, sc in each of next 13 sc, hdc in each of next 11 sc, sc in each of rem 10 sc: 61 sts.

Rnd 5: Sl st in first sc, sc in next sc, inc in next sc, sc in next sc, sl st in each of next 26 sts, sc in each of next 5 sc, sl st in each of rem 26 sts; finish off: 62 sts.

SIZES MEDIUM & LARGE ONLY

Rnd 4: Sc in first sc and in each of next (16-17) sc, dc in each of next (12-13) sc, sc in each of next 15 sc, dc in each of next (12-13) sc, sc in each of rem (11-12) sc: (67-71) sts.

Rnd 5: Sl st in each st around entire sole; finish off.

TOP

With **right** side facing, smaller size hook and **single strand** Ecru, join with sl st in center of heel; ch 2 **(counts as hdc)**.

Rnd 1: Working in back loop only, hdc in each sl st across; join with sl st in 2nd ch of beg ch-2; ch 1, **turn**: 62(67-71) hdc.

Rnd 2: Sc in first hdc and in each hdc across; join with sl st in beg ch-1 taking care not to work an extra st in joining of prev row; ch 1, turn.

Rnd 3: Sc in first sc and in each sc across; join with sl st in beg ch-1; ch 1, turn.

Rnd 4: Sc in first sc and in each of next 26(30-32) sc, dec in next 2 sts as follows: pull up a loop in each of next 2 sts, YO and draw thru all 3 loops on hook **(dec made)**, (sc in next sc, dec) 2(1-1) time(s), sc in each of rem 27(31-33) sc; join with sl st in beg ch-1; ch 1, turn: 59(65-69) sc.

Rnd 5: Sc in first sc and in each of next 25(28-30) sc, dec, sc in each of next 3 sc, dec, sc in each of rem 26(29-31) sc; join with sl st in beg ch-1; ch 1, turn: 57(63-67) sc.

Rnd 6: Sc in first sc and in each of next 25(28-30) sc, dec, sc in next sc, dec, sc in each of next 26(29-31) sc; join with sl st in beg ch-1; ch 1, turn: 55(61-65) sc.

Rnd 7: Sc in first sc and in each sc across; join with sl st in beg ch-1; finish off.

TOP INSERT

Row 1: With **right** side facing, smaller size hook and **single strand** Dk Blue, join with sl st in 26th(29th-31st) sc from center of heel; sc in same sc, sc in each of next 3 sc; ch 1, turn: 4 sc.

Row 2: Sk first sc, sc in each of next 3 sc, sc in each of next 2 sc on side ***(Fig. 4)***; ch 1, turn: 5 sc.

Fig. 4

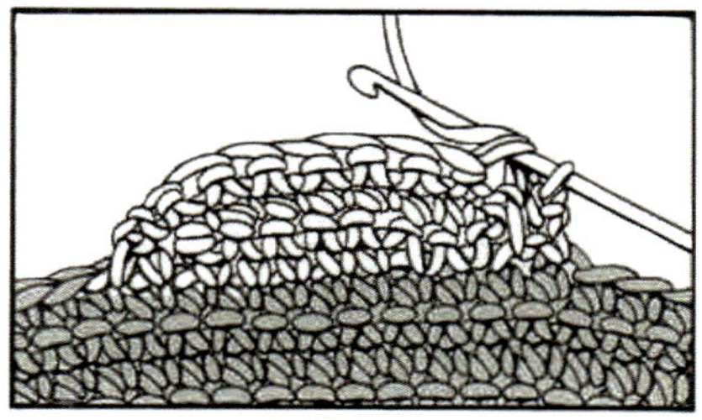

Row 3: Sk first sc, sc in each sc of Insert, sc in each of next 2 sc on side; ch 1, turn: 6 sc.

Rows 4-7: Rep Row 3, 4 times **more**: 10 sc.

SIZE SMALL ONLY

Row 8: Sc in first sc and in each sc across; finish off.

SIZES MEDIUM & LARGE ONLY

Row 8: Sk first sc, sc in each sc of Insert, sc in each of next 2 sc on side; ch 1, turn: 11 sc.

Row 9: Sc in first sc and in each sc across; finish off.

FINISHING

EDGING

With **right** side facing, smaller size hook and **single strand** Dk Blue, join with sl st in center of back; ch 1, sc in each sc around; join with sl st in beg ch-1; finish off.

In center of Top Insert, with Lt Blue and Lazy Daisy Stitch ***(Fig. 5)***, embroider one 8-petal flower. With Dk Blue work French Knot ***(Fig. 6)*** in center of flower.
Weave in any yarn ends.

Fig. 5

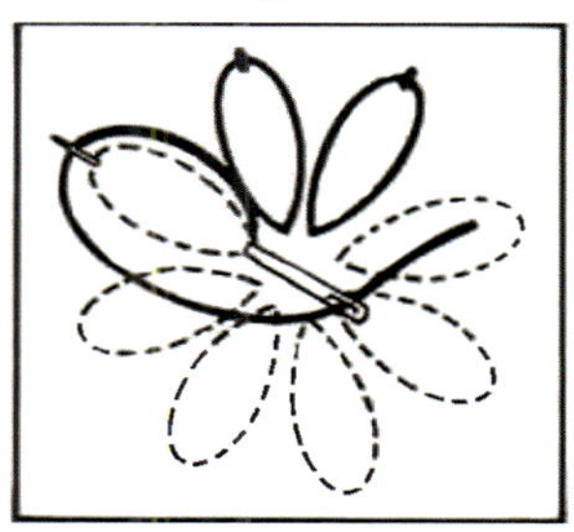

Fig. 6

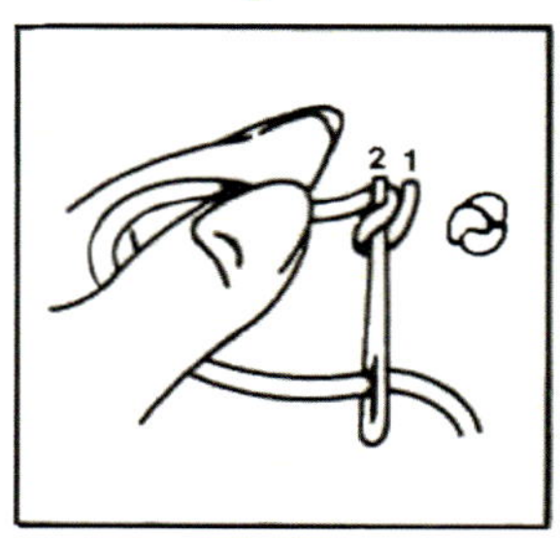

CHILDREN'S SIZES: SMALL MEDIUM LARGE

	SMALL	MEDIUM	LARGE
	7½"	8"	8½"

Size *Note*: Instructions are written for smallest size with changes for larger sizes in parentheses.

MATERIALS

Worsted wt yarn –
- 1(2-2½) oz [approx 28.4(56.8-71) grams] Dk Blue
- 1(1-1½) oz [approx 28.4(28.4-42.6) grams] Ecru
- 3 yards Lt Blue

Aluminum crochet hook –
- Size E (3.5 mm) **for Top only**
- Size G (4.5 mm) **for Sole only**
  or sizes needed for gauge

Tapestry or yarn needle

GAUGE: Size E hook, 16 sc and 16 rows = 4"
Size G hook (double strand),
14 sc and 14 rows = 4"

INSTRUCTIONS

SOLE (Make 2)

With larger size hook and **double strand** Dk Blue, ch 18(20-22) **loosely**.

Rnd 1: Work 3 sc in 2nd ch from hook, sc in each of next 7(8-9) chs, dc in each of next 8(9-10) chs, 5 dc in last ch (toe); turn piece to work in each unused loop of foundation ch, dc in each of next 8(9-10) loops, sc in each of rem 8(9-10) loops; mark beg of rnd with contrasting yarn **(now and throughout)**: 39(43-47) sts.

Rnd 2: Work 2 sc in first sc **(inc made)**, inc in next sc (heel), sc in each of next 16(18-20) sts, inc in each of next 5 dc at toe, sc in each of rem 16(18-20) sts: 46(50-54) sc.

Rnd 3: Inc in first sc, sc in next sc, inc in next sc, sc in each of next 17(19-21) sc, (inc in next sc, sc in next sc) 4 times, inc in next sc, sc in each of rem 17(19-21) sc: 53(57-61) sc.

SIZE SMALL ONLY

Rnd 4: Sc in first sc and in each sc around; finish off: 53 sc.

SIZES MEDIUM & LARGE ONLY

Rnd 4: Sc in first sc and in each of next (14-15) sc, hdc in each of next (10-11) sc, sc in each of next 13 sc, hdc in each of next (10-11) sc, sc in each of rem (9-10) sc; finish off: (57-61) sc.

TOP

With **right** side facing, smaller size hook and **single strand** Ecru, join with sl st in center of heel, ch 2 **(counts as hdc)**.

Rnd 1: Working in back loop only, hdc in each st across; join with sl st in beg ch-2; ch 1, **turn**: 53(57-61) hdc.

Rnd 2: Sc in first hdc, sc in each hdc across; join with sl st in beg ch-1 taking care not to work an extra st in joining of prev row; ch 1, turn.

Rnds 3 and 4: Sc in first sc and in each sc across; join with sl st in beg ch-1; ch 1, turn.

Rnd 5: Sc in first sc and in each of next 23(25-27) sc, dec in next 2 sts as follows: pull up a loop in each of next 2 sts, YO and draw thru all 3 loops on hook **(dec made)**, sc in next sc, dec, sc in each of rem 24(26-28) sc; join with sl st in beg ch-1; ch 1, turn: 51(55-59) sc.

Rnd 6: Sc in first sc and in each of next 21(23-25) sc, dec, sc in each of next 3 sc, dec, sc in each of rem 22(24-26) sc; join with sl st in beg ch-1; ch 1, turn: 49(53-57) sc.

Rnd 7: Sc in first sc and in each of next 21(23-25) sc, dec, sc in next sc, dec, sc in each of rem 22(24-26) sc; join with sl st in beg ch-1; ch 1, turn: 47(51-55) sc.

Rnd 8: Sc in first sc and in each sc across; join with sl st in beg ch-1, finish off: 47(51-55) sc.

TOP INSERT

Row 1: With **right** side facing, smaller size hook and **single strand** Dk Blue, join with sl st in 23rd(25th-27th) sc from center of heel; sc in same sc and in each of next 3 sc; ch 1, turn: 4 sc.

Row 2: Sk first sc, sc in each of next 3 sc, sc in each of next 2 sc on side ***(Fig. 4, page 9)***; ch 1, turn: 5 sc.

Row 3: Sk first sc, sc in each sc of Insert, sc in each of next 2 sc on side; ch 1, turn: 6 sc.

Rows 4-7: Rep Row 3, 4 times **more**: 10 sc.

SIZE SMALL ONLY

Row 8: Sc in first sc and in each sc across; finish off.

SIZES MEDIUM & LARGE ONLY

Row 8: Sk first sc, sc in each sc of Insert, sc in each of next 2 sc on side; ch 1, turn: 11 sc.

Row 9: Sc in first sc and in each sc across; finish off.

FINISHING

EDGING

With **right** side facing, smaller size hook and **single strand** Dk Blue, join with sl st in center of back; ch 1, sc in each sc around; join with sl st in beg ch-1; finish off.

In center of Top Insert, with Lt Blue and Lazy Daisy Stitch ***(Fig. 5, page 9)***, embroider one 8-petal flower.
With Dk Blue, work French Knot ***(Fig. 6, page 9)*** in center of flower.
Weave in any yarn ends.

5. CRISSCROSS SANDALS

Shown on back cover

designed by Marian Brodman

WOMEN'S SIZES:	SMALL	MEDIUM	LARGE
	9"	9½"	10"

Size *Note*: Instructions are written for smallest size with changes for larger sizes in parentheses.

MATERIALS

Worsted wt yarn – 4½(5-5½) oz
[approx 127.8(142-156.2) grams] Med Gold
Aluminum crochet hook – Size G (4.5 mm)
or size needed for gauge
1 sheet plastic canvas, 10½" x 13½"
Tapestry or yarn needle

GAUGE: With double strand of yarn,
14 sc and 16 rows= 4"

INSTRUCTIONS

Note: Use double strand throughout.

SOLE (Make 4)
Ch 22(25-27) **loosely**.

Rnd 1: Work 3 sc in 2nd ch from hook, sc in each of next 9(10-11) chs, dc in each of next 10(12-13) chs, 5 dc in last ch (toe); turn piece to work in each unused loop of foundation ch, dc in each of next 10(12-13) loops, sc in each of rem 10(11-12) loops; mark beg of rnd with contrasting yarn (**now and throughout**): 47(53-57) sts.

Rnd 2: Work 2 sc in first sc **(inc made)**, inc in next sc (heel), sc in each of next 20(23-25) sts, inc in each of next 5 dc at toe, sc in each of rem 20(23-25) sts: 54(60-64) sc.

Rnd 3: Inc in first sc, sc in next sc, inc in next sc, sc in each of next 21(24-26) sc, (inc in next sc, sc in next sc) 4 times, inc in next sc, sc in each of next 21(24-26) sc: 61(67-71) sc.

CHILDREN'S SIZES: SMALL MEDIUM LARGE

	SMALL	MEDIUM	LARGE
	7½"	8"	8½"

Size Note: Instructions are written for smallest size with changes for larger sizes in parentheses.

MATERIALS

Worsted wt yarn – 3(3½-4) oz
[approx 85.2(99.4-113.6) grams] Med Gold
Aluminum crochet hook – Size G (4.5 mm)
or size needed for gauge
1 sheet plastic canvas, 10½" x 13½"
Tapestry or yarn needle

GAUGE: With double strand of yarn,
14 sc and 16 rows = 4"

INSTRUCTIONS

Note: Use double strand throughout.

SOLE (Make 4)

Ch 18(20-22) **loosely**.

Rnd 1: Work 3 sc in 2nd ch from hook, sc in each of next 7(8-9) chs, dc in each of next 8(9-10) chs, 5 dc in last ch (toe); turn piece to work in each unused loop of foundation ch, dc in each of next 8(9-10) loops, sc in each of rem 8(9-10) loops; mark beg of rnd with contrasting yarn **(now and throughout)**: 39(43-47) sts.

Rnd 2: Work 2 sc in first sc **(inc made)**, inc in next sc (heel), sc in each of next 16(18-20) sts, inc in each of next 5 dc at toe, sc in each of rem 16(18-20) sts: 46(50-54) sc.

Rnd 3: Inc in first sc, sc in next sc, inc in next sc, sc in each of next 17(19-21) sc, (inc in next sc, sc in next sc) 4 times, inc in next sc, sc in each of next 17(19-21) sc: 53(57-61) sc.

SIZE SMALL ONLY

Rnd 4: Sc in first sc and in each of next 15 sc, hdc in each of next 11 sc, sc in each of next 13 sc, hdc in each of next 11 sc, sc in each of rem 10 sc: 61 sts.

Rnd 5: Sl st in first sc, sc in next sc, inc in next sc, sc in next sc, sl st in each of next 26 sts, sc in each of next 5 sc, sl st in each of rem 26 sts; finish off: 62 sts.

SIZES MEDIUM & LARGE ONLY

Rnd 4: Sc in first sc and in each of next (16-17) sc, dc in each of next (12-13) sc, sc in each of next 15 sc, dc in each of next (12-13) sc, sc in each of rem (11-12) sc: (67-71) sts.

Rnd 5: Sl st in each st around entire sole; finish off.

STRAPS (Make 4)

Ch 17(18-19) **loosely**.

Row 1: Sc in 2nd ch from hook and in each ch across; ch 1, turn: 16(17-18) sc.

Row 2: Sc in each sc across; ch 1, turn.

Rows 3 and 4: Rep Row 2, twice; at end of Row 4, do **not** ch 1.

Finish off.

FINISHING

Cut 2 pieces of plastic canvas each ¼" less around than shape of sole.
Insert one piece plastic canvas between 2 soles placed **wrong** sides together. Sew 2 soles together.
Cross 2 straps and sew to each sole, placing straps to hold foot securely.
Weave in any yarn ends.

SIZE SMALL ONLY

Rnd 4: Sc in first sc and in each sc around; do **not** finish off.

SIZES MEDIUM & LARGE ONLY

Rnd 4: Sc in first sc and in each of next (14-15) sc, hdc in each of next (10-11) sc, sc in each of next 13 sc, hdc in each of next (10-11) sc, sc in each of rem (9-10) sc; do **not** finish off: (57-61) sts.

ALL SIZES

Rnd 5: Sl st in each st around entire sole; finish off.

STRAPS (Make 4)

Ch 15(16-17) **loosely**.

Row 1: Sc in 2nd ch from hook and in each ch across; ch 1, turn: 14(15-16) sc.

Row 2: Sc in each sc across; ch 1, turn.

Rows 3 and 4: Rep Row 2, twice; at end of Row 4, do not ch 1.

Finish off.

FINISHING

Cut 2 pieces of plastic canvas each ¼" less around than shape of sole.
Insert one piece plastic canvas between 2 soles placed **wrong** sides together. Sew 2 soles together.
Cross 2 straps and sew to each sole, placing straps to hold foot securely.
Weave in any yarn ends.

6. SCRAP SLIPPERS

Shown on front cover

designed by Joyce Shelton
Pine Needlecraft, Litchfield, MN

WOMEN'S SIZES:	SMALL	MEDIUM	LARGE
	9"	9½"	10"

Size *Note*: Instructions are written for smallest size with changes for larger sizes in parentheses.

MATERIALS

Worsted wt yarn – 4½(5-5½) oz
[approx 127.8(142-156.2) grams] Scrap colors
Aluminum crochet hook – Size H (5.5 mm)
or size needed for gauge
Tapestry or yarn needle

GAUGE: With double strand of yarn,
12 sc and 12 rows = 4"

INSTRUCTIONS

Note: Use double strand throughout.
Colors may be changed at random.

SOLE (Make 2)

Ch 7(7-8) **loosely**.

Row 1: Sc in 2nd ch from hook and in each ch across; ch 1, turn: 6(6-7) sc.

Row 2: Work 2 sc in first sc **(inc made)**, sc in each sc across; ch 1, turn: 7(7-8) sc.

Rows 3-5: Inc in first sc, sc in each sc across; ch 1, turn: 10(10-11) sc.

Next 7(9-11) Rows: Sc in first sc and in each sc across; ch 1, turn.

Dec Row: Dec in next 2 sts as follows: pull up a loop in each of first 2 sc, YO and draw thru all 3 loops on hook **(dec made)**, sc in each rem sc across; ch 1, turn: 9(9-10) sc.

Next 2 Rows: Rep Dec Row twice **more**; 7(7-8) sc.

Next Row: Sc in first sc and in each sc across; ch 1, turn.

Repeat previous row until Sole measures 8½(9-9½)".

Dec Row: Dec, sc in each sc across to rem 2 sc, dec; ch 1, turn: 5(5-6) sc.

Rep last Dec Row once **more**; do **not** ch 1, finish off: 3(3-4) sc.

TOP (Make 2)

Ch 8(8-9) **loosely**.

Row 1: Sc in 2nd ch from hook and in each ch across; ch 1, turn: 7(7-8) sc.

Row 2: Working in back loop only ***(abbreviated BLO)***, inc in first sc, sc in back loop of each sc across; mark for **right** side with contrasting yarn; ch 1, turn: 8(8-9) sc.

Next 11(13-14) Rows: Working in BLO, inc in first sc, sc in BLO of each sc across; ch 1, turn: 19(21-23) sc.

Next 2 Rows: Sc in BLO of first sc and in each sc across; ch 1, turn.

SIDES

Row 1: Working in BLO, sc in first sc and in each of next 6(7-8) sc; ch 1, turn.

Row 2: Working in BLO, sc in first sc and in each sc across; ch 1, turn: 7(8-9) sc.

Repeat Row 2 for 11 rows **more or** until length is sufficient to reach center back of Sole.
Finish off.

Join yarn with sl st in 6th sc from side just worked; sc in back loop of same sc and in each of rem 6(7-8) sc across; ch 1, turn.

Work in same manner as first side.
Finish off.

FINISHING

Sew back seam of Sides.
Position Top so that center st of Top toe matches center st of Sole toe, and back seam of Sides matches center st of Sole heel. Sc thru both thicknesses around Sole; finish off.
Weave in any yarn ends.

CHILDREN'S SIZES:

SMALL	MEDIUM	LARGE
7½"	8"	8½"

Size Note: Instructions are written for smallest size with changes for larger sizes in parentheses.

MATERIALS

Worsted wt yarn – 3(3½-4) oz
[approx 85.2(99.4-113.6) grams] Scrap colors
Aluminum crochet hook – Size H (5.5 mm)
or size needed for gauge
Tapestry or yarn needle

GAUGE: With double strand of yarn,
12 sc and 12 rows = 4"

INSTRUCTIONS

Note: Use double strand throughout.
Colors may be changed at random.

SOLE (Make 2)

Ch 6(6-7) **loosely**.

Row 1: Sc in 2nd ch from hook and in each ch across; ch 1, turn: 5(5-6) sc.

Row 2: Work 2 sc in first sc **(inc made)**, sc in each sc across; ch 1, turn: 6(6-7) sc.

Rows 3-5: Inc in first sc, sc in each sc across; ch 1, turn: 9(9-10) sc.

Next 6(7-8) Rows: Sc in first sc and in each sc across; ch 1, turn.

Dec Row: Dec in next 2 sts as follows: pull up a loop in each of first 2 sc, YO and draw thru all 3 loops on hook **(dec made)**, sc in each rem sc across; ch 1, turn: 8(8-9) sc.

Next Row: Rep Dec Row once **more**: 7(7-8) sc.

Next Row: Sc in first sc and in each sc across; ch 1, turn.

Repeat previous row until Sole measures 7(7½-8)" or ½" less than desired length.

Dec Row: Dec, sc in each sc across to rem 2 sc, dec; ch 1, turn: 5(5-6) sc.

Last Row: Sc in first sc and in each sc across; finish off: 5(5-6) sc.

TOP (Make 2)

Ch 7(7-8) **loosely**.

Row 1: Sc in 2nd ch from hook and in each ch across; ch 1, turn: 6(6-7) sc.

Row 2: Working in back loop only ***(abbreviated BLO)***, inc in first sc, sc in back loop of each sc across; mark for **right** side with contrasting yarn; ch 1, turn: 7(7-8) sc.

Next 10(10-11) Rows: Working in BLO, inc in first sc, sc in BLO of each sc across; ch 1, turn: 17(17-19) sc.

Next 2 Rows: Sc in BLO of first sc and in each sc across; ch 1, turn.

SIDES

Row 1: Working in BLO, sc in first sc and in each of next 5(5-6) sc; ch 1, turn.

Row 2: Working in BlO, sc in first sc and in each sc across; ch 1, turn: 6(6-7) sc.

Repeat Row 2 for 8(9-11) rows **more or** until length is sufficient to reach center back of Sole.
Finish off.

Join yarn with sl st in 6th sc from side just worked; sc in back loop of same sc and in each of rem 5(5-6) sc across; ch 1, turn.

Work in same manner as first side.
Finish off.

FINISHING

Sew back seam of Sides.
Position Top so that center st of Top toe matches center st of Sole toe, and back seam of Sides matches center st of Sole heel.
Sc thru both thicknesses around Sole; finish off.
Weave in any yarn ends

7. FLOWER BALLERINA

Shown on front cover

designed by Mary A. Watkins; Little Rock, AR

WOMEN'S SIZES:	**SMALL**	**MEDIUM**	**LARGE**
	9"	9½"	10"

Size Note: Instructions are written for smallest size with changes for larger sizes in parentheses.

MATERIALS

Worsted wt yarn – 4½(5-5½) oz
[approx 127.8(142.5-156.8) grams] Maroon
Aluminum crochet hook – Size H (5.5 mm)
or size needed for gauge
Tapestry or yarn needle

GAUGE: 16 hdc and 8 rows= 4"

INSTRUCTIONS (Make 2)

Ch 38(40-42) **loosely**.

Row 1: Working in back loop only ***(abbreviated BLO)***, hdc in 3rd ch from hook, hdc in each of rem 35(37-39) chs; ch 2, turn: 36(38-40) hdc.

Row 2: Working in BLO, hdc in first hdc and in each hdc across; ch 2, turn.

Rows 3-18: Rep Row 2, 16 times **more**; at end of Row 18, do not ch 2.

Finish off leaving a 36" length.

FINISHING

Fold piece in half lengthwise.
Holding both edges at top tog, sc with 36" length thru both edges, working in one loop only of each st, for 4".
Sew heel end tog.
Baste across toe end, gather end closed and tie knot in basting yarn.
Weave in any yarn ends.

FLOWER
Ch 24.

Row 1: Dc in 4th ch from hook, ★ ch 2, sk next ch, dc in next ch; rep from ★ across, ending by working dc in last ch; ch 1, turn: 11 dc.

Row 2: Work 5 dc in first ch-2 sp **(petal made)**, ★ sc in next dc, 5 dc in next ch-2 sp; rep from ★ across, ending by working 5 dc in turning ch, sc in other end of first dc of prev row; finish off, leaving a 23" length for sewing: 11 petals.

Holding last petal worked with **right** side facing, wrap rem petals **loosely** around ***(Fig. 7)***. With 23" length and tapestry needle, sew flower securely to top of slipper. Weave in any yarn ends.

Fig. 7

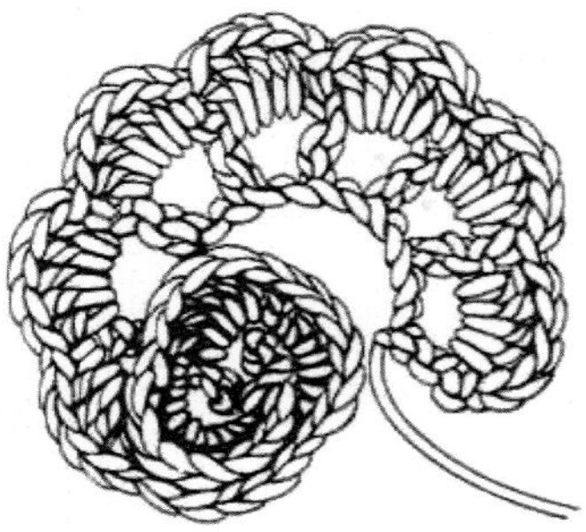

CHILDREN'S SIZES:

	SMALL	MEDIUM	LARGE
	7½"	8"	8½"

Size Note: Instructions are written for smallest size with changes for larger sizes in parentheses.

MATERIALS

Worsted wt yarn – 3(3½-4) oz
[approx 85.5(99.4-113.6) grams] Maroon
Aluminum crochet hook – Size H (5.5 mm)
or size needed for gauge
Tapestry or yarn needle

GAUGE: 16 hdc and 8 rows= 4"

INSTRUCTIONS (Make 2)
Ch 32(34-36) **loosely**.

Row 1: Working in back loop only ***(abbreviated BLO)***, hdc in 3rd ch from hook, hdc in each of rem 29(31-33) chs; ch 2, turn: 30(32-34) hdc.

Row 2: Working in BLO, hdc in first hdc and in each hdc across; ch 2, turn.

Rows 3-16: Rep Row 2, 14 times **more**; finish off leaving a 36" length.

FINISHING
Fold piece in half lengthwise.
Holding both edges at top tog, sc with 36" length thru both edges, working in one loop only of each st, for 4".
Sew heel end tog.
Baste across toe end, gather end closed and tie knot in basting yarn.
Weave in any yarn ends.

FLOWER
Work same as for Women's Sizes.

Instructions tested and cover items made by JoAnn Bowling, Janet L Duell, Irene Espy, Kate Fitzpatrick, Virginia Hogan, Christel Shelton, Modene Thornton, Annie Mary Wilson.

Made in U.S.A.